THINGS TO DO IN HELL

THINGS TO DO IN HELL

Chris Martin

COFFEE HOUSE PRESS
Minneapolis
2020

Coffee House Press books are available to the trade through our primary distributor, Consortium Book Sales & Distribution, cbsd.com or (800) 283-3572. For personal orders, catalogs, or other information, write to info@coffeehousepress.org.

Coffee House Press is a nonprofit literary publishing house. Support from private foundations, corporate giving programs, government programs, and generous individuals helps make the publication of our books possible. We gratefully acknowledge their support in detail in the back of this book.

LIBRARY OF CONGRESS CATALOGING-IN-PUBLICATION DATA

Names: Martin, Chris, 1977 August 11– author.
Title: Things to do in hell / Chris Martin.
Identifiers: LCCN 2020019669 (print) | LCCN 2020019670 (ebook) | ISBN 9781566895958 (trade paperback) | ISBN 9781566896016 (ebook)
Subjects: LCGFT: Poetry.
Classification: LCC PS3613.A77785 T48 2020 (print) | LCC PS3613.A77785 (ebook) | DDC 811/.6—dc23
LC record available at https://lccn.loc.gov/2020019669
LC ebook record available at https://lccn.loc.gov/2020019670

PRINTED IN THE UNITED STATES OF AMERICA
27 26 25 24 23 22 21 20   1 2 3 4 5 6 7 8

The pains of heaven
are with me

and the pleasures of hell
are with me

CONTENTS

THINGS TO DO IN HELL

EPILOGUE

We ate the pigs out of compulsion

We ate the dogs next, as radiated fish piled

Like sandbags at the ocean's edge

We ate the cats, the caterpillars, the pill bugs

We feasted on bright-white ants' eggs

We fasted

We slowed

We sowed brittle barren seeds and reaped nothing

We owed everything

We wed neglect

We'd

ZEALOUS

I am alive at night I am
alive between cities I am alive

crossing from fear to regret
I am alive during the broadcast I

am alive eventually I am alive for
the moment I am alive gazing

and glowing at this window's edge I am
alive how and why I am alive in the uncertain

hands of another I am alive just
as the haunch of a listening horse

trembles I am alive kind of like you
are alive except entirely different I am

alive like a rumor or mirror I am alive
mostly at night I am alive nowhere

but as I am named I am alive only
slightly I am alive pawed and whiskered I

am alive quiet in the pause
between elegies I am alive right

away I am alive sudden and insatiable
I am alive to those who hold me

with necessary desperation I am alive
unless I am not I am alive very nearly always

at night I am alive whereas the faceless
reader is too alive I am alive exactly

the way a wild spinach leaf is
alive I am alive you know I am alive

zealous in my hunches

PALINODE

Dying out, dying in
A crowd of impossible people
Seed back to swagger
Of concussive light

A crowd of impossible people
In the generalized insolence
Of concussive light
A bedraggled bee priest

In the generalized insolence
Until stumbling on purpose became a kind of dance
A bedraggled bee priest
Calling this song appropriate fever

Until stumbling on purpose became a kind of dance
And scraping clues from the sloughed eggshell of zero
Calling this song appropriate fever
As melody spools loose

And scraping clues from the sloughed eggshell of zero
Courting not what coheres
As melody spools loose
Minus batteries, bladder full, excess arteries

Courting not what coheres
We follow only putrefaction
Minus batteries, bladder full, excess arteries
Pickled and fetal in a slow formaldehyde waltz

We follow only putrefaction
All of our plural in the surge and blur
Pickled and fetal in a slow formaldehyde waltz
I will love you more

All of our plural in the surge and blur
While at home like a sold flower
I will love you more
In fits of unpaid disavowal

While at home like a sold flower
A circle whose center is everywhere
In fits of unpaid disavowal
And crashing down with heaven's offal

A circle whose center is everywhere
I want to be serrated
And crashing down with heaven's offal
Prowling an ersatz horizon

I want to be serrated
Licking a speckled fender
Prowling an ersatz horizon
Where the you finally becomes *you*

Licking a speckled fender
With pagan longing
Where the you finally becomes *you*
In a library where the dead crest on waves of pelvic light

With pagan longing
They called it a poem
In a library where the dead crest on waves of pelvic light
Horrifying the merest fact into choreography

They called it a poem
Where an evening cloud stains the nasturtiums
Horrifying the merest fact into choreography
She asked me to hold her like an octopus

Where an evening cloud stains the nasturtiums
Posting torrid flowers of true rage
She asked me to hold her like an octopus
At the world's wet, unfinished edge

Posting torrid flowers of true rage
The guy at the bodega
At the world's wet, unfinished edge
Is asking what's safer

The guy at the bodega
Compulsively parts
Is asking what's safer
To be the sword or

Compulsively parts
The curtain of his lip
To be the sword or
The flesh opening a way forward

The curtain of his lip
In the vibration between selves
The flesh opening a way forward
To accumulate in a spare room

In the vibration between selves
Aggregate pulse
To accumulate in a spare room
The hundred billion stairs blood walks in silence

Aggregate pulse
Tricking pauses into cinema
The hundred billion stairs blood walks in silence
Knowing we could say anything now

Tricking pauses into cinema
Time is one fucked-up dude
Knowing we could say anything now
Fledged between cracked marble

Time is one fucked-up dude
Like a willow huffing rat breath in a half-frozen field
Fledged between cracked marble
This country is leaving this country

Like a willow huffing rat breath in a half-frozen field
A hymn is what we most resemble
This country is leaving this country
Nothing but rhythm

A hymn is what we most resemble
In his deepest red and flaming robe
Nothing but rhythm
I came apart and they called it laughing

In his deepest red and flaming robe
A little object spoke
I came apart and they called it laughing
My hand on your back in the opening to the cave

A little object spoke
My ear so far
My hand on your back in the opening to the cave
As the world's curl fucks against you its faceless beaming fuck

My ear so far
A stranger's parade
As the world's curl fucks against you its faceless beaming fuck
Through floating columns of nuclear trash

A stranger's parade
Night is a general condition
Through floating columns of nuclear trash
And braced against the dub waves

Night is a general condition
The doctor said I was exhausting it
And braced against the dub waves
Or aroused by plainer virtue

The doctor said I was exhausting it
Unbearable money
Or aroused by plainer virtue
A tongue where the flaws of language stand out, pale and beaded

Unbearable money
Between resting and resisting a little *is* is
A tongue where the flaws of language stand out, pale and beaded
And cut with squatter's milk

Between resting and resisting a little *is* is
To allow brighter office in day's mistake
And cut with squatter's milk
We shake awake our worn cosmos

To allow brighter office in day's mistake
With faces that rename
We shake awake our worn cosmos
A habitat for love of talking

With faces that rename
Dying out, dying in
A habitat for love of talking
Seed back to swagger

YES THE ANIMALS

In my arid philosophy in my blue
blossom of fear in my can't

face another day without the consolations
of cinema in my drought in my east

facing turret in my face clawing
at its mask in my goodnight nurse

in my herpetology and rigor mortis in
my I can't face another night minus

entwinement in my jealousy for the dead
in my knit and furrow in my lurid

anamnesis in my made and unmade
faith in my nemesis the groveling fork

in my of and between in my purl
and splinter in my questions etched

where even I cannot travel in my ravel
and spill in my serial catastrophes

in my ten final minutes before the sun
scatters us like flies in my unmade

faith become license in my vapid
philosophy in my exeunt prolonged

in my yes the animals and only
the animals will answer

to this woe

THINGS TO DO IN HELL

Grab lunch
Polish your silver
Try a new flavor of yogurt
Burn in a lake of fire
Smoke some weed
Overeat

Finally understand some things
Talk to Steve
Cry out breathlessly
Pay the electric bill
Go to the aquarium in the mall
Worry over the shape and color of your moles

Sell out the people you used to call friends
Learn how to bake bread
Feed the ducks at the lake by the highway
Exaggerate your assets
Get elected
Mull things over

Attend a livestock auction
Pull down the statues of people who tortured your ancestors
Seek employment
Knit
Regret mostly everything
Paint the windows shut

Pull down the statues of your ancestors
Get down on your knees
Read Kierkegaard
Pick the kids up from Montessori
Lose your appetite
Linger

DVR *Homeland*

Imagine that hell is only an abstraction

Take another free breath mint

Cry out endlessly

Blame those closest to you

Love even the barest light pissing through the trees

EXIT

The animals asked and asked and
were not quiet the animals behaved

in predictable ways so we might
understand the animals came

at night to see what remained
the animals decimated by belief

the animals each and every
the animals followed the aftershock

toward safety the animals got
what we deserved the animals hung

from power lines in the permanent
brownout the animals in cages

could only watch the animals
just over the seawall the animals

knew and they were not quiet
the animals listened in the pause

between screaming the animals made
adept by catastrophe the animals never

stopped moving the animals only slept
when the moon was new the animals

prodded the silent heaps the animals
quick and deliberate the animals restive

at night the animals sought complexity
and avoided clearings the animals to

the right and left the animals underneath
the burning highway the animals vole

and weasel watching the animals exit
like breath from the manholes at dawn

WALKING TOUR OF AN IMAGINARY HOMELAND

The airplane inside us was running out of pretzels

We took the drugs in the morning so we could see at night

All day clinging to ghastly seaweed on the naked internet ocean

We thought, okay, neglect equals geography

As our habits grew unrecognizable so far from the strobe

And cold menace of a quivering *if*

What I didn't say was I was worried you might think

I was fine but insufficient

A total dick with wet cuffs like Zebulon Pike

In the vacuum of night

I can almost smell all these leases expire

Leashes?

Softening in the efflorescent decay tenure

And crippled in near-attainment

But less here already

We sipped unlegislated self-light like half-sour breast milk

Midlife is a drop ceiling

The future like a lake of cooling bacon fat

Computers do it for us anyway

Unless we tell them not to

Which we won't

WOUND

Like breath after the dark wave
unwinds you from its arms like breath

below the hearing of a near hunger like
breath caught in the barbed hollow

of a barely open throat like breath doesn't care
if the breather is ready like breath escapes

through the divot of a chipped tooth
like breath fleshes January air like

breath given a long and red leash like
breath here in the wet cave we call

prelude like breath in between earth
and paw like breath jarred in the spiraling

scar of vinyl like breath knitting each
frayed silence into cause like breath

lit by a capillary swell like breath mustered
and armed like breath nodding off on

its apneal yo-yo like breath of fawns
hiding in sunlight's dapple like breath pulling

cottonwood seeds from a lover's hair
like breath questioning what it lets

in like breath remained its own answer
like breath surgical and quick like breath

threaded between the words of a nursery
rhyme like breath undone by the trees

that have come to love expiration like breath
vast as a planetless sky like breath wound

around the hasty thorn of death

AN OUROBOROS OF TRUE FORGIVENESS

Cluster-un-fucked, suddenly, and without explanation

The parts of you flaking off don't have to make peace with it

A split-level universe with no owner

She called him Worry or Sorry, I could never remember

Recipes for clotted milk, haphazard seduction, a diminutive tic

The future is all he ever seems to cry about

When it was finally over they just started *over* over again

Living together in a sufficiency called Languor

It peeled and peeled until the peel was *it*

Where love means leaving

Piles of vitamins on the kitchen table

Tragic crevice

Graphic device

All the dead celebrities discovered by fathers younger than we are now

Postprandial transit, invisible river

All your former lovers taking a do-over

The selected poems were more like endless briar

John thought I said we shit the snow globe

I don't care I'm going to love you until my name reverts to a word

VICIOUS THIS

Around the apple core around the bitten
seed around the cinder block around

the deepest arid well around the epithet
unearned around the face-to-face

attempts at reconciliation around the give
and take around the height I am now

around the I I was then around the jilt
and flee around the kerosene-lit oil drum

around the lumps and abrasions around
the morning I last heard that fool

bird's brazen crow around the nether
night makes available around the orchid

you drew into my shin around the pavement
piled around the quince tree's barren

squander around the riffraff we call
family gathered around the smaller and

smaller table around the time we stopped
counting days around the urchin's

tentative shine around the vicious this
is why this is why this is why this is

WALKING TOUR OF WE NO LONGER LIVE INSIDE THE WHALE

Wrong decisions in the shower are louder than airplanes

A few misguided leaves practicing fortitude

Simon thought I was talking about cartoons

I thought he was talking about cryo

Where the solid world glows sold for culture

Walking with no given purpose, even the birds knew to avoid her

Plowing lower

Neighborhood known only as WE GROW TO HATE OUR OWN PETS

What doesn't change is longing to get fucked up

They found the membership in his small intestine

It was broken the moment you bought it

Duct-taping the mouth of the oracle shut

Total wowzers

I tried to feed it back through the mechanism

First it got worse, then it got better, then it tried to kill me

Ego thin as an eyelash or pendulous like baleen

Depends on the vintage

I ate only what they put before me

All the snow in Hollywood

UNIFIED

This is why airplanes keep disappearing this
is why blue was the final color this is why

disappearance is a pill resembling police this
is why even now I cannot find an appropriate hue

to speak of my face this is why final words
need to be written this is why glow and tangle

this is why hands are shaped like leaves this
is why I cup creek water over the horizon

of your lip this is why justice is hoarse this is
why knowing is not enough this is why lists

tend to bloat the subject this is why my
hands are turning purple this is why nothing

can swallow airplanes this is why other colors
rush to the wound this is why people

leave this is why question after question left
his mouth like a strange parade this is why red

was the first color this is why some people
come back this is why the ocean only truly turns

blue when it's a desert this is why unified
field theory won't save us

SECRET MENU

Christian Nape

Fox in the Snow in the Bar in the Dark

Sunk Cost

Everyone You'd Thought to Ask Is Suddenly Elsewhere

Joseph Beuys Buys the Seraph a Fernet

Ash on the Black Leash

Hotel Laughter

Where Our Love Grows Like a Profusion of Bog Lilies

Innardly

Like Whale Fall to the Bristleworm

Orlando Woolridge

Starting with the Coda

Natural Attic Light

I Want You to Hold the Amulet While I Carry You over the River

THE NEXT DAY AND THRUM

I am alive at dawn I am alive because
I am quick I am alive cast in the bronze

light of a November sick I am alive
deep in the recesses of a dark ark I am

alive every time death forgets to breathe
I am alive for just a few real moments

I am alive gut and angle I am alive high
above the scrap heap I am alive if living is

the opposite of ease I am alive jowl
and grit I am alive knee to spleen I am

alive low in the animal hum I am alive
more like a wave than a particle I

am alive now that the superfluous
parts of me aren't I am alive or

I am a symptom of aliveness others curate
into stark recognition I am alive pacing

the temporary autonomous zone I am
alive quick against the hush I am alive red

livered and warm in the pulverized dreg I
am alive so that the dead might be nightly

sung I am alive the next day and thrum
through each braided strand of my sorrow

BREAKUP MIXTAPE

Breaking up still felt like breaking in

The thought that everything could be ours

A closet where you recite what's necessary but impractical

Voice bathed in wool

Carbon copy of ardent longing

I wanna break up with this century

A cemetery for horses

Who told you it was okay to make currency a dial tone?

Tiny untraceable molecules that loved you anyway

Cracked earth harboring its perfect skulltop architecture

The words he repeated most

Were the ones he couldn't understand, like *hallelujah*

Embracing the glue shortage

An amnesia memorialized in consumer choices

Our living ossuary

Where the door is too swollen to close

Songs you only revisit when the night's over for everyone else

SAYS I

The next day announces itself like a headline
without a story the next day bores up

through a fault in the government plaza
the next day comes quiet as phosphorescence

around our ankles the next day decimates
the wreckage so we can begin again the next

day eases each of us into the boil we call
future the next day forgives all we promised

in the desperate pause of night the next day
glowers like an injured toad the next day hangs

itself on principle the next day is far less
than it was imagined to be the next

day joins pageant to sergeant the next
day knows exactly what it is doing

wrong the next day limps into the sunrise
like a child refusing to die the next day

means the batteries will probably fail the next
day never comes the next day opens its patient

jaws like a bottom dweller expecting bounty
the next day pleads and the next day questions as

the next day reads in stunned silence the shifting
prophecy that appears the next day says

it's difficult to look upon us without a face
that says *I cannot promise you anything but pain*

ITTERS

Wanting to know

But not wanting to Google it

Pure juice of loss

The Top 40 offered to be his sex therapist

A kryptonic geometry where curves are really muted corners

Telling me about you so you can ask me about *it*

We drove headlong into a wall of gospel pop

Groin meadows

Illustrated companion to a domestic sex adventure

Where the it became itter

REALLY

It's as difficult as remembering
not to breathe it's become difficult

to metaphorically sketch the parameters
of pain it's clearly difficult for a single person

to articulate it's difficult in the sense that
it's possible it's difficult even when the least

obstruction has been removed it's forming
difficult alliances it's grown difficult

to separate the shadow from the forecast
it's hardly difficult to see it's in difficulty

that we trace the will's eel-like glow it's just
difficult it's killingly difficult to breathe it's less

difficult if you know that pain has
a terminus it's more difficult if

you perceive the sun as a predator and not
a comfort I mean it's not difficult it's impossible

it's only difficult in the sense that an alternative
occurs to you it's placing difficult words

in the crowded mouth of hope it's quite difficult
to imagine it's really difficult to forget if you

become one of the few that manages to survive it

IF YOU LIVED HERE YOU'D BE DEAD ALREADY

Gym clout of a star interrogator

Tell the program I don't want it to understand my face

Hurtling toward entropy in someone else's glove compartment

And other boring torture dreams

Gangsta rap wedged between my chest and the BabyBjörn

She dismissed it as hypercapitalist insurrection

But what if everything's a mouth?

Another Nextdoor panopticon

Your neighbor's Christmas lights banging a double-parked Benz

Surgically unpunctual

The previews used to be my favorite part

Agitating for the freedom to be asleep

Managing the hunger of those who must be starved

I'm not calling the cops the cops are calling me

QUICKLY IF NEVER

To forget a life in the midst of
living it to forget barest smoldering

details to forget cause and see only
effect to forget details that don't

smolder to forget everything that isn't
charred to forget for every child the world

before its arrival to forget grace
without apocalypse to forget

his name but not his smell to forget it
all to forget just enough to forget knowing

how to remember to forget less or
to forget more as the tide of survival

varies to forget names but not desire
to forget or forgive what could not be

avoided to forget prayer but continue
praying to forget quickly if never

completely if never compliantly

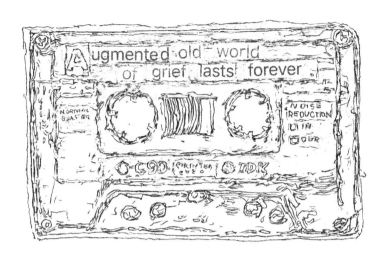

NOT A FEW WANDER HOMELESS ON DARKSOME PATHS

Sleep isn't death it's diet psilocybin

To wake in a field of consequence and brittle leaves

Feet are alien sculpture

A story I tell myself about other people's equity

Silence isn't clarity it's obstruction

Terrible tiny decisions I imagine my intelligent friends also make

A hesitation nest

Where feeling better means refusing instruction

I went to the river but the river was just cold wind through a birch crotch

Dying up

Nomadic desire of the preposition

I admit it I assumed you were too attractive to be virtuous

A blue sofa covered in wet snow

Indomitable realism

An invisible room in the subfloors of Hotel Wentley

I'd take us over shitty heaven any day

You came into my life to change it and it did so and that's that

PAST

If never asked the name you carried before
the disaster if never before the sun

went down if never came like a postman
with empty arms if never deepened

like eels under December ice if never
for the right reasons if never God's

chosen people if never herald but always
hind if never inside the kingdom if

never just a foot inside the kingdom if
never knack but always scrape if never let

be or alone if never made from abalone
or pearl if never nerve but always

riven like a shell if never only came
once if never past the apology's

opening note

EVERYTHING ELSE

I keep thinking about that day in San Francisco

When I gave wrong directions to the hospital

And expired zoo attractions

Walking around in someone else's backyard

In the middle of the night on purpose?

So high I thought this is what RoboCop must feel like

As Sunnylyn copped us bottle after bottle

When I woke up my hands were around the fire extinguisher so I went home

Far too much Manhattan

Far too little everything else

The stolen dog barked for a week and then resumed a cheerful oblivion

It was all in the present tense, even the regret

Broken salad

A cordage of gassy brain vine

I ate whatever they put before me and left when joy demoded

When they said turn left, they meant turn over

Never having read hospitality in the forest

Before everything in the Village went Froyo & Chase

Before money was money

As we moved forward we held hands

And to many it appeared that we were searching for a missing child

OWNS EVEN THE SLOW

The apology arrives out of breath
to an empty house the apology grows

thin and viscid like a graft applied
to the eye's ravaged fascia the apology

cries at the kitchen table while animals
gather at the windows the apology does

whatever the tragedy requires the apology
eyes itself suspiciously the apology flattens

and packs our collective pain into a sharp yet
bearable density the apology grows thinner and loses

muscle tone and sleeps late the apology has no time
to imagine its flaws or their opposite the apology

keeps the matriarch from taking the lessons
of grief to her grave untaught the apology jostles

the fish of complicity loose from the line the
apology keeps us hungry amid the glut the

apology lingers especially where it is refused
the apology might come in the form of animal

flesh the apology nests wherever it can find
an appropriate lapse the apology owns

even the slow unfurling of our tangled fingers

DÉNOUEMENT

There was some confusion

Regarding the uncertain distinction between art and hat

I climbed into a hole

By which we chose to represent our squandered earning potential

It was surprisingly warm

And smelled like the absence of operative language, rotting lilac

Success is the lowest art, wrote Anselm

As the capacious brain of the mountain patiently wastes

Its genius on us

Whose eyes are on a different planet than our ears

But hold your breath for several years

And you can hear one syllable of cosmic gossip

Unwind

I practice my mineral mind

And angle my neck to the air like a western-facing crag

I could stop my metabolism entirely

But the golden age of television keeps streaming at ungodly speeds

NEVER BY

Even the armadillos swayed like brazen
gunslingers through the black hush

even the barest cloud arrived like moment's
curdled miracle even the cold of an un

earthed stone even the decimation danced
in the rippling heat even the ever-lit

refinery pulling shadows from the arroyo
like puppets even the five mange-met

puppies blind in the cellar even the gold
less valuable than milk even the hue

of a yucca spear even the is that isn't
quite there even the jut of hunger

on an ox's taut hip even the knowledge
that husbandry is what got us here

even the list of sins dwarfed by predation
even the mistakes and even the never

by then dwarfed by a never ever

A GAME IN WHICH LOSING IS INCONSEQUENTIAL

You start by choosing sides

Visa or Mastercard, Doritos or Cheetos

But then the sides multiply

Cool Ranch or Cooler Ranch

You get to pick from the mystery pile every time you forget your age

You can fall in love with a typo if you're not careful

Falling in hate requires only minimal humiliation

You win, you lose, you find what's lost, you lose

The will to continue, you continue

Cooler Ranch or Jacked 3D Jalapeño Pepper Jack

As redundancy finds itself conducive to holistic entanglement

It's a cut 'n' paste life y'all

With apostrophes where our eyes used to be

Abraded controller thumbs and tight leather sweatpants

You choose *and* you lose

You love so hard you forget the score

There is a child in the other room telling a walrus what morning is

LECTURE ON WESTERN MUSIC

Music is organized sound in time

Beaten, plucked, blown, struck

It is always changing or staying the same

In addition to rhythm there is a hidden tessitura

The register at which an instrument finds its ideal timbre

Being a cave for music my body

Resonates comfortably in certain registers

On airplanes I feel a buoyant tessitura

While others feel their strings fraying toward snap

And when strangers applaud at marathons

Tessitura overwhelms me to tears

A single thrumming audience

Multiplied and apart

Rhythm is the placement of events in time

But could it also be their effacement?

Sometimes so much

Happens in the rush just to appear

The events meld continuous

On the sustained note of a broken chord

And, being continuous, my body

Doesn't reveal its deepest rhythm

Except when we stand so close

Our stomachs touch

Effaced at their curve

Tessitura when you make

The same *hnnh*

That rappers make

Between lyrics

Against my collarbone

A BIG HUNGRY US

First we got married for the insurance

Then we got married like The-Dream, just to throw a party

We listened to The-Dream on every road trip

His voice on "Culture" like a velvet hand caressing moss

Took out the IUD, took up diabetes

The baby wanted to press all that sugar into flesh

So we took a winter walk after every meal

Or sometimes you did alone

Pendulous on Iowa ice, especially at night

Baby pounding the uterus taut

Dome life

We devoted ourselves to *Buffy*

and *The Next Generation*

Commander Deanna Troi

Carried a ball of light

To term in only three days

Orgasmic birth, half-Betazoid

In our yearning, our hearing, but never

Our earning

We watched and re-watched

The Filipino wraith's

Rendition of Whitney's Dolly

Love in perpetuity

As the performer repeatedly births

Ghoul after ghoul, knowing love

In perpetuity is always monstrous

The due date came and then dissolved

We had three days to dissolve with it

Your water broke at midnight

And everything broke open

But not before we signed their horrifying waivers

And your thigh tremored like a steering wheel at 120 mph

We held a thousand pulsing sculptures

Together against the waves

While night flagged and shifts changed

Coalescing always under the sign of bravery

Eos & ice chips

In the radiant strobe between waiting and wailing

You were so there you were not there

Pulling from the deep well

Leavening pain with an immense, blazing resolve

And time was not the case

Until Atticus was

All folds and blood and need

Though he didn't cry at his circumcision

Only later when they returned him to my arms

And despite the mundane fearmongering

He slept beside us

Endangered by our need and fatigue

A big hungry us

Convalescing cloud forming bravery's shade

In a bed for strangers

And when the hospitality was over

I jury-rigged the car seat

Drove illegally slow

Forgot the placenta

And drove back illegally fast

AC blasting to keep it frozen

He was so white

He was bald for almost two years

We moved north

And bought white-cotton pre-folds

We moved into a duplex with built-ins and a finished basement

And lived deep into the white months of milk and spit

We moved Atticus into his own room

And the clipped hairs under my lower lip turned white

A big hungry us

Endangered by need and fatigue

Flopping exhausted on the brittle shag

Culling the first cut curl

Filling up

Our slowly unrolling white scroll

With love and mistakes

DECIDUOUS HYMN

Light listens at his body busy

Worlding itself

Into a Wednesday, an afternoon

GLOWINGROWING

As the two begin to coincide

Cinder and cell

Cleaving from fire's trunk

Its momentary prong of flame

A dense orthography

Where acicular leaves

Fall into my book

Flooding it with countless hims

Versions and visions

Viscous light bent around the splotch

Of his parti-bruised knee

Viscous light working

Drunk around

The sun-tight curve of each curl

Ripe light looking to

Thread vertebrae, sleeve muscle

The whole body swollen, grown

Monstrous in its bloom

He teems, light

Listens, I

Write to catch

Some reflected instance

Of world in word

As it falls away, remaining

Strangely full, I write

To describe some low hum of built him

By dint of its glow, its deep

And denticulate kindling

A SMALL HUMAN BEING BREAKS EVERYTHING

He wants to break

the television, wants to

break the book's dry yellow

spine. He breaks the butter

dish, fills our hearts as if

he were pouring stained glass

into a mold. When they set

he breaks them, just to see

scatter and shine. He

literally doesn't know any

better. He's breaking

free of my hand, planting

unsteady feet on just-opened

flowers. We dub him the Prince

of Destruction and he opens

one eyeball wide as a saucer

before smashing it under delicate

blond-tipped lashes. He breaks

our common language so we might

remember how to read

its entrails. The guts of the day

splay over the slow-spreading night

and we slip into bed, break

into our dreams with one pickax

of hot breath after another.

Only a few hours and he breaks

the unfinished cinema of sleep

with a wail, breaks his eyes open

with hunger and loneliness. We can't

hold anything together except

love, which grows even

as it breaks, like an exploded

beer's antic and stationary laugh

dazzling the freezer. Smiles

break open on our suddenly ancient

faces, broken ever and always

with the wonder of being still

alive, too alive, almost

broke, breaking each day as

a way to stay whole.

MY UNGODLY

By then a single knock meant the dogs
had gathered by then birch leaves had been

plastered onto the doors of safe houses
by then children knew how to imitate the call

of every nocturnal bird by then demons
circulated like weary tourists by then everyone

was whittling their handful of hope down
to fate by then saints had grown rampant by

then highway exits appeared to hover over
the water like concrete docks by then

I only knew the names of a dozen undead
by then jellyfish were lapping at the shoreline

like the sea had gone rabid by then killing
could no longer pass as sacrifice by

then little else could be done by then
my ungodly hands held nothing but will

FLAGS OF SURRENDER

white as I

white as lye

white as lilies

white as silicone

white as oblivion

white as the emperor
of ice cream

white as spilled milk

white as spider silk

white as a ghost

white as bleach

white as blood

white as pus

white as ash

white as rabid

white as flight

white as knights

white as blinding

white as snow

white as now

white as no

LESSON

What ungodly animals are we what
ungodly billowing does this brain

make against the spirit what ungodly
calm this morning assembles the stage

for what ungodly drama tonight
and what ungodly ear erases the free

music of the forest what ungodly
forgetting has been allowed the helm

what ungodly god swallows the flesh
what ungodly hollow have we dug

in our thirst what ungodly instrument
of anxious desire what ungodly justice is

this endless shiver what ungodly knowledge
is this shiver's blur what ungodly lesson

do I imagine in its exaggerated blue

AFTER DAWN

What is the sound of

Unending firsts

Bursting against the face, the sound

Of the asterisk, the exception

Breaking the sun?

On a small farm we call self

We fail, accumulate, little mouths

That wound over with salve.

We inhabit brutal days

Where it is impossible not

To look askew, though heaven knows

I've seen you try. I heard

What's worse, the broken bray, sloughing

What's cosmic for mere comedy

As if life were its own

Genre. The masks, they said, were for

Our protection. Hours. Missive

Caught between the expired liquicaps of

Dayquil we call teeth. White as shit.

Solution: a daisy

From which darker love is demanded.

for and after Dawn Lundy Martin

KNOWING I STILL DON'T

Imagine a magazine full of airbrushed
bullets whizzing by imagine blinking twice

meant to release the arrow imagine
coming up through the throat of another

pink-slashed morning imagine dew
softening your wounds imagine *easy now*

whispered in your ear like one would whisper
to a spooked horse imagine forgetting

how to imagine God's wrath imagine He
burns through the skull of the earth

like a migraine imagine if each surviving text
were a single neuron imagine jeremiads

thrown like flint against the stone of all
the disappeared imagine knowing I still don't

know how now exits the wet mouth of what

PAIN AND MERCY

A desire larger than me but also pulsing

Right through my particular diode

Crushing soft, crushing hard

And caught in the accordion of distant suns

We slowly decompose in an instant

Remains?

Cross-eyed time & bogus acres

Buying in & dying out

Belching forth a thousand brand names in a cold stupor

Where every breakbeat tells us the soul

Of the worker would rather

Rage and wage

Psychedelic emancipation

But instead, you know, friable tiles

From the dome of hegemony

Sift gold dust on our aching scalps

The masters tell us we're not food

Experience tells us different

Now take this harness and the toxic clemency of pointless labor

And circulate

The year an intersection and each season a moving quadrant

Busting donuts

In a car made of pain and mercy

Which is love and love's shadow

A glow where the penumbral edge swipes tomorrow

I once worked quality check in a swab factory

I still can't afford California

My son tells me he's "chopping hands to build a tree"

On this airplane that glows over Kansas City

Hi Anne!

But California can't afford California

JUMP FROM FLY

I still don't know the name of this flower
I still don't know best I still don't know cater

from neuter I still don't know dolomite
from limestone I still don't know everything

my child needs me to I still don't know
formal words for all the parts of my body

that are failing I still don't know go
from leave I still don't know how I am

going to breathe outside this door I
still don't know jump from fly

THIS IS JUST TO SAY

As long as you promise

to walk with me

into whatever they call

the next hell

I will be okay

even if they call it heaven

HONEY

I am alive and the stone is
listening I am alive because you are

tending the blisters on my hands I am
alive cauterized and nurturing

endless jars of sauerkraut I am alive
drowsy in my ghast I am

alive even when I am forced to live
on castoffs and grist I am alive

feral and fermented I am
alive gift after gift after I am

alive handing your last word
back to you like honey in a spoon

IT'S LIKE THEY ALWAYS SAY

I couldn't say

Someone has to say something

Say it don't spray it

What you say can be held against you

Just say it

If you don't say it I will

You can't just say something like that

What did you just say?

Say whatever comes to mind

Say it again

Oh my god, what are we even saying?

Are you saying what I think you're saying?

I say we do it

One day you can say you were there

They say that don't they?

You know what I'm saying?

Never say never

Say what?

Say yes

Say anything

I can't say it enough

for and after Stephanie Gray

GASP THE REASON

Your last asteroid of joy
immolating before impact your

last bed before the journey
whose end can only be

guessed at your last cauliflower
and kohlrabi your last diffidence

sloughed like a démodé dress
your last Earth your last

fistula leading the survived like
pus toward air the last gasp

the reason I've been keeping
my stolid shuffling lungs empty

BRIGHTER OFFICE IN DAY'S MISTAKE

If *the future is whatever administrates*

our concupiscence in the present

somehow Mary and I have taken

to calling Atticus "The-Future," only half joking

but also frightened by the way parenthood is so

administrated, administrative

The-Future bounding through the living room

tripping over a lamp, screaming, crying, bounding

elsewhere, while our concupiscence waits

like a minivan before the blinking X

of an endlessly snaking train

what doesn't change is wanting

to get fucked up

administrating derangement

against all that packages the day

only to find derangement itself

made orderly like a beer-of-the-month club

so also frightened by capitalism

and trying to explain morality to The-Future

without choking on the gristle

of meaningless ideology we've been

stuffed with, his stuffed fox under us

as we tour our apartment

The-Future's knees tucked up behind the long ears

as I scoot us over the hardwood floors

and past the mirror, where lately

he's been practicing sadness

his face warping in furrows and droops

a sculptural act that leaves him truly blue

privileged to practice, I suppose

but there are real tears and they sprout

silent down his cheeks and just today

he got caught between practicing

his smile and his scowl

having oscillated so quickly they merged

into an antic and pulsing rictus

I asked him what his face was now

and he said Mad-Happy

FORGET HOW TO SPEAK

The reason I answered the phone
is that it hadn't rung in months the reason

I began my studies is that I couldn't stop
turning the various endings over

in my mind the reason I couldn't breathe
seemed linked to my fear of doors

the reason I demanded light be allowed
to cascade from the roof into the courtyard

was obvious to the mothers the reason
I entered the nursery so often was that I

craved the chorus they made laboring
to wake the reason I forget how

to speak when the animals are
gathering is that I am trying to be

an animal who remembers how
peace makes the kill possible

ANSWERS

Whether a trifle or a necessary

quotient of now, I can't stop

America from overflowing

its river of costumes, thousand-

banked where the final me bursts

plural in a tomb of its own

making. So of course I wonder

whether we need another

book of poems by another

cis-straight-white Roth IRA

who resembles everything

he has come to resent.

And then I immediately want

to see that question in print.

Thank the devil poetry isn't

about answers, isn't minions

shopping orthodoxy while

the money rolls in. Answers

are whatever bursts in

plain sight: the falling

acorn; hot, black buffalo

tongue; thrum

of the cicada; gait of

the beloved returning from

afar—even *the nearest gnat is*

an explanation, a frenzied period

looking for the page, a world-

shaped answer. Poetry is about more

than about, its hands reaching

out like an octopus trapped

in a wallet. Camouflage, ink, the ply

of a restless form that simmers

with chromatophores, metaphors

that don't pause for us

to read them

to death, swipe

and frame, pin

and post, stop. There is a child

in the rubble, a pension in the hands

of a whimsical billionaire, a bundle

of estranged rage occupying

the Planned Parenthood

and killing indiscriminately.

And what does it mean that I don't

have to tell you that the man was

a man. That I don't have to

say it was a white man shooting

people who should not be shot

in an office dedicated to women's health.

So I understand if you have fantasies

of women shooting up marble offices

where pinstriped men watched over

by placid abstracts perpetuate

their silently violent economies. Me

too. And it doesn't change

the fact that our house rule is no

guns, even imaginary, even if

the television keeps trying to hand

our son trigger after trigger, far

before he can hope

to understand what they are. I want

the poets and priests to switch places, want

Y-chromosomes to be the new

exclusion for firearm ownership, want

a million-dollar equity ceiling and free

preschool, a phalanx

of neighbors facing the police

facing each other. When Tito

reads a draft of this poem, he replies

with an answer in question's drag—

what is the brim of want

and what is the trough.

EXCEPT

I am alive after all I am
alive but the floating dander

of the dying stings my nostrils I
am alive centipede after gnat

I am alive down where the tunnels
still smell of bisphenol I am

alive except I hear nothing but
the give of bruised fruit

Y

because convenience is the stepladder to oblivion

because X was murdered in the Audubon Ballroom

because calamity demands risk

because spiritual crisis is the B-side to privilege

because silence is obstruction

because one kind of equity is mute and the other is deafening

because a wave of dim hush pushes the violence forward

because no one can void the face's blank membership card

because O.K. is what we say when it's anything but

because the foundation of every dream is rot

because the bitterest crop is the most abundant

because plunder is the very air

because melanin density hampers the conversion of sunlight into vitamin D

because the aliens aren't coming soon enough

because my people were pagan AF before the Romans showed up

because the cops keep letting me talk them out of it

because resisting only turns to resting when a big fucking *is* breaks free

DEEPEN

I hear nothing and its wet
throb I hear nothing burrow

and shiver like a lone vole I hear
nothing choosing a nest

within zero's dense yolk I
hear nothing deepen

YRUOK

Another day made of acetate and other people

The melting pot in a meltdown

And I see you flossing a gray Lexus SUV

Toward the cooling towers of delusion

Extreme makeovers & gerrymandered hearts

With tweets where the silent pauses used to go

Look: the sky itself winces

The ocean pulls back in revulsion

The meltdown is way, way down

But petrochemical disaster stocks skyrocket

And the masks become, what, our faces?

Siphoning gigs from an oversize data splay

I wore the same expression for years

Until I realized how white it was

A sheen of normative aspects you shed and repair

I actually *loved* the president

And he was, like, smoking cigarettes and killing people

All of human society caught in the glitch between levels

Some of us dying out, some of us dying in

Reading philosophy with the lights off

My woes swimming backstroke in a sea of likes

My eyeballs not so much glued as abraded

Building an oneiric retreat shell for the snail of your tongue

And corroding into a brackish hush

Even love is agitation

Is a fielding of the agitation

Even love is the fielding

Of an agitation-that-worlds

CURDLED LIKE ALL

The writing absolved only
those willing to see it

as a consolation for light
the writing broke through

the very wall it was hoping
to name the writing cradled

under our fingers curdled
like all we were doing

was waiting for the dough
of grief to be proved

In the circle whose center is everywhere

I grasp a quaking fish, a hand in the dark water

Pulling it taut like I could mark

Brethren among these loose tatters of blather

Each scale a kindness and protection

Against the sour and too-sure

Teeth of cowardly swagger

In the circle whose center is everywhere

My ear opens sideways like an empty pocket

Unreasonably full and refusing

To let our hands be parted

We bask and grow inside its spill

Snow on snow, stars expiring, the obscene

Squeal each city bus's brakes make

Creaky plank in the nursery, hoarse cough

At the microphone of justice

In the circle whose center is everywhere

The humming buzz

Of the one who listens

Is never silent

In the circle whose center is everywhere

You work at the thorn

Rubbing it blunt

The thorn of jealousy, of oblivion

You scrub the invisible thorn of whiteness

Until its point is obliterated

You abrade all that juts

Spear-tip sharp from the split

Lips of those who gather and scavenge

On the poor, the wounded, the lost

In the circle whose center is everywhere

There is a forest of refusal

And the names of those who resist

Ease, stupor, silence, and greed

Are listed among the trunks

Which are full from top to root

And the forest is the earth

In the circle whose center is everywhere

A man who is a girl who is a bear

Lets their hair grow until the wars are over

And it spills out in yellow vines

Over the cracked skin of the earth

As they stretch to meet each other

Under the never-ending war

Whose marquee is the sky

In the circle whose center is everywhere

We sheep

We bear

We flea

We clover

We silt

And till where the earth gurgles

With a blood both dizzy and mute

We till and pile, ply and shape

Until the statues of our grief sleeve the river

Until the architecture of our regret

Threatens to dwarf the very peaks

Which have always showered us

With a clear and perfect pity

In the circle whose center is everywhere

The snowmen are multiplying but

In the circle whose center is everywhere

The future is not white

The future is not straight

And the future sure as hell

Does not belong to man, or men, or anyone

Who would secretly cower behind the curtain of force

In the circle whose center is everywhere

The future is black and belongs to the squid

In the circle whose center is everywhere

The future is queer and carries children in its mouth

In the circle whose center is everywhere

The future chooses

Fold over sword and song over word

In the circle whose center is everywhere

The future is free and belongs

To the fungi, the algae, the bacteria

Braided coursing chemical epic

Whose singing will go on long

After our tongues return to soil

Seeking obligation

In the circle whose center is everywhere

We are the color of leather, of wood

Worn from constant touching

We are the color of spoiled milk

And secondhand shoes

The color of bones piled and moldering

In the circle whose center is everywhere

We are the color of light bulbs just extinguished

And a brittle winter hydrangea leaf

In the circle whose center is everywhere

We are the color of rain-fed dirt

In the circle whose center is everywhere

The horizon holds us

Like a simmering liquid

Seeking edge

And when we exceed containment

And radiate toward the unseen

When we are moved by love

Of all we don't know

The circle moves with us

In the circle whose center is everywhere

We are building an outer ring of nitrogen and ice

To house the bodies of the men

Who practice passive murder in the name of profit

In the circle whose center is everywhere

We are reinventing anguish

Our mouths wide

Like the outstretched wings

Of a gliding vulture

As you cup salvaged water

Over the endless parade

Made of our lips

In the circle whose center is everywhere

We watch as the richest and poorest of us

Sprawl and stack and prowl

Porous and perforated schist

Looking for crude

We watch as they ingurgitate the earth

With contraptions built to hack and claw

And burn a dwindling bounty

In the circle whose center is everywhere

I want most to turn

Du Bois's scalpel

Against the whole

Of humanity

But first of all

Myself

How does it feel

To be

A problem?

BORE

Like all we ate became the silver
lining of a self-consuming snake like

all we bore along the throb-notches
in our spines became the design

of something far more intelligent

FIFTY SHITTY HEAVENS

Hand-me-down heaven
Nicorette heaven
Heaven of the feculent couch flower
Bread heel heaven
Heaven of the totaled asset

Nearly okay heaven
Easy-bake heaven
All-you-can-eat-buffet heaven
Heaven of baseless empires
Heaven of mishandled communion wafers

Crawlspace heaven
Heaven of racist umpires
Febreze heaven
Fluorescent heaven
Crown-on-every-asshole heaven

Obstructed view heaven
Heaven of the botched hand job
Sublet heaven
AP heaven
Minimum heaven

Heaven of shaking hands with the boss's boss
Bedbug heaven
Free market heaven
Heaven of counsel and liability
Uneven heaven

Layover heaven
Heaven of the overpaid philanderer
Abandoned fraggle heaven
Staycation heaven
Sext heaven

Heaven of the forgone conclusion
Heaven of the revolving department chair
Inedible heaven
Peterbilt heaven
Heaven of the dormant threat

Heaven of the harmless left
House-arrest heaven
Clever heaven
Heaven of the curdled epiphany
Stand-your-ground heaven

Heaven of the drowning adjunct
Rent-to-own heaven
Meth heaven
Heaven of the middling blur
Heaven of the eighteen-month sleep regression

Maximum-security heaven
Redline heaven
Heaven that white people like
Heaven of meager and desperate solace
Heaven of eager compliance

AND

I'm dying and apricots
sneeze open where they fall

PREFACE

We

We awe

We weave

We weave even the awe of grief

into the eaves of our makeshift cities

We waver in the awful air of having

been bought

We awe at having been brought

so low

We wake to the slow voice

of earth turning

We awe that the worms are weaving

their blind and endless song

and know we owe everything to the churn

We awe at how we owe and so

we song and song and song

NOTES

The epigraph is a reversal of Whitman.

"Zealous" took its initial inspiration from Siah Armajani's exhibition *Follow This Line* at the Walker Art Center. Mary Austin Speaker took me to the exhibition on a date, indulged in some collaborative writing, and was crucial in helping me determine the larger abecedarian structure.

"Palinode" is a reversed version of an abandoned poem that was excised, line by line, from an abandoned manuscript and assembled by Daniel Poppick.

"Things to Do in Hell" was born from a conversation I had with a student. I've written a separate essay, "The Healing Power of Poetry," on how that conversation led to the poem's composition. It can be found on the website Please Kill Me. I also discuss the poem on a PoetryNow podcast.

"Walking Tour of an Imaginary Homeland," and many other poems in this book, are indebted to the work of my dear friend Simon Evans. This book is dedicated to him.

"Not a Few Wander Homeless on Darksome Paths" takes its title from a phrase of Heidegger's. The poem concludes with a hat-tip to Ted Berrigan's "Red Shift."

"Everything Else" is dedicated to Sunnylyn Thibodeaux and Micah Ballard.

I wrote "Lecture on Western Music" while literally attending a webinar on Western music.

The ghoulish performance referenced in "A Big Hungry Us" can be found by using the search terms "creepy whitney lip-synch."

"After Dawn" is written in the echo of a poem by Dawn Lundy Martin, to whom it is also dedicated. The solution in the poem's final lines comes from Paul Celan.

"Brighter Office in Day's Mistake" begins with a quotation from Brandon Brown.

In "Answers," *the nearest gnat* comes from Whitman. Tito is the poet and memoirist Tito Mukhopadhyay.

"Y R U O K" concludes with a reference to the writing of Erin Manning.

The war hair in "In the Circle Whose Center Is Everywhere" belongs to CAConrad.

"Fifty Shitty Heavens" is an homage to a work by Simon Evans entitled *Shitty Heaven*. The poem was commissioned by Hanne Lippard for an exhibition of hers at the Goethe-Institut and performed on escalators in the skyways along-side Mary Moore Easter, Miriam Karraker, and Lara Mimosa Montes.

"And" and all the reverse abecedarian poems in this book take great inspiration from Inger Christensen's nuclear abecedarian *alphabet*.

ACKNOWLEDGMENTS

Earlier forms of these poems first appeared in *The Portable Boog Reader, Elderly, Nine Mile,* and on the Poetry Foundation website.

Lines from "Palinode" are culled from poems that first appeared in the Academy of American Poets' Poem-a-Day series, the *Agricultural Reader, All Small Caps, BPM,* the *Brooklyn Review, Critical Quarterly, Epiphany,* the *Equalizer, Esque, Greetings, High Chair, Krispy Kremes, Mrs. Maybe, Notnostrums,* the PEN Poetry Series, *Sea Ranch, Sink, They Will Sew the Blue Sail, Try!, Turntable,* and *VLAK.* They were also culled from a chapbook, *enough,* published by Ugly Duckling Presse.

I want to thank Soren for the first seed.

I want to thank Daniel Poppick for salvaging the hymns and interlocuting my thoughts on all things heaven and hell.

I want to thank Erika Stevens, Carla Valadez, Marit Swanson, Daley Farr, and Chris Fischbach at Coffee House Press for their guidance, attention, insight, commitment, and friendship.

I want to thank Li-Young Lee for his willingness to debate the relative merits and likelihood of heaven (his) and hell (mine).

I want to thank Hanif Abdurraqib, Angela Pelster-Wiebe, Timothy Otte, Ben Polk, and especially Mary Austin Speaker for being this book's first readers.

I want to thank Simon Evans for twenty years of distant intimate friendship, and I want to thank both him and Sarah Lannan for endowing this body of words with an infernal face and organs.

Coffee House Press began as a small letterpress operation in 1972 and has grown into an internationally renowned nonprofit publisher of literary fiction, essay, poetry, and other work that doesn't fit neatly into genre categories.

Coffee House is both a publisher and an arts organization. Through our *Books in Action* program and publications, we've become interdisciplinary collaborators and incubators for new work and audience experiences. Our vision for the future is one where a publisher is a catalyst and connector.

Funder Acknowledgments

Coffee House Press is an internationally renowned independent book publisher and arts nonprofit based in Minneapolis, MN; through its literary publications and *Books in Action* program, Coffee House acts as a catalyst and connector—between authors and readers, ideas and resources, creativity and community, inspiration and action.

Coffee House Press books are made possible through the generous support of grants and donations from corporations, state and federal grant programs, family foundations, and the many individuals who believe in the transformational power of literature. This activity is made possible by the voters of Minnesota through a Minnesota State Arts Board Operating Support grant, thanks to the legislative appropriation from the Arts and Cultural Heritage Fund. Coffee House also receives major operating support from the Amazon Literary Partnership, Jerome Foundation, McKnight Foundation, Target Foundation, and the National Endowment for the Arts (NEA). To find out more about how NEA grants impact individuals and communities, visit www.arts.gov.

Coffee House Press receives additional support from the Elmer L. & Eleanor J. Andersen Foundation; the David & Mary Anderson Family Foundation; Bookmobile; Dorsey & Whitney LLP; Foundation Technologies; Fredrikson & Byron, P.A.; the Fringe Foundation; Kenneth Koch Literary Estate; the Matching Grant Program Fund of the Minneapolis Foundation; Mr. Pancks' Fund in memory of Graham Kimpton; the Schwab Charitable Fund; Schwegman, Lundberg & Woessner, P.A.; the Silicon Valley Community Foundation; and the U.S. Bank Foundation.

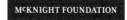

The Publisher's Circle of Coffee House Press

Publisher's Circle members make significant contributions to Coffee House Press's annual giving campaign. Understanding that a strong financial base is necessary for the press to meet the challenges and opportunities that arise each year, this group plays a crucial part in the success of Coffee House's mission.

Recent Publisher's Circle members include many anonymous donors, Patricia A. Beithon, the E. Thomas Binger & Rebecca Rand Fund of the Minneapolis Foundation, Andrew Brantingham, Dave & Kelli Cloutier, Louise Copeland, Jane Dalrymple-Hollo & Stephen Parlato, Mary Ebert & Paul Stembler, Kaywin Feldman & Jim Lutz, Chris Fischbach & Katie Dublinski, Sally French, Jocelyn Hale & Glenn Miller, the Rehael Fund-Roger Hale/Nor Hall of the Minneapolis Foundation, Randy Hartten & Ron Lotz, Dylan Hicks & Nina Hale, William Hardacker, Randall Heath, Jeffrey Hom, Carl & Heidi Horsch, the Amy L. Hubbard & Geoffrey J. Kehoe Fund, Kenneth & Susan Kahn, Stephen & Isabel Keating, Julia Klein, the Kenneth Koch Literary Estate, Cinda Kornblum, Jennifer Kwon Dobbs & Stefan Liess, the Lambert Family Foundation, the Lenfestey Family Foundation, Joy Linsday Crow, Sarah Lutman & Rob Rudolph, the Carol & Aaron Mack Charitable Fund of the Minneapolis Foundation, George & Olga Mack, Joshua Mack & Ron Warren, Gillian McCain, Malcolm S. McDermid & Katie Windle, Mary & Malcolm McDermid, Sjur Midness & Briar Andresen, Daniel N. Smith III & Maureen Millea Smith, Peter Nelson & Jennifer Swenson, Enrique & Jennifer Olivarez, Alan Polsky, Robin Preble, Alexis Scott, Ruth Stricker Dayton, Jeffrey Sugerman & Sarah Schultz, Nan G. Swid, Kenneth Thorp in memory of Allan Kornblum & Rochelle Ratner, Patricia Tilton, Stu Wilson & Melissa Barker, Warren D. Woessner & Iris C. Freeman, and Margaret Wurtele.

For more information about the Publisher's Circle and other ways
to support Coffee House Press books, authors, and activities,
please visit www.coffeehousepress.org/pages/donate
or contact us at info@coffeehousepress.org.

CHRIS MARTIN is the author of four books of poetry and the recipient of grants from the Mellon Foundation, the National Endowment for the Arts, and the Minnesota State Arts Board. He is the cofounder and executive director of Unrestricted Interest, an organization dedicated to helping neurodivergent learners transform their lives through writing. He lives in Minneapolis, where he professes at Hamline University and Carleton College.

Things to Do in Hell was designed by
Bookmobile Design & Digital Publisher Services.
Text is set in Arno Pro.